Quality by Delitala (QbD)
Volume 1:
The Quality Manual

By: Michael A. Delitala

Dedicated to Jefferey T. Jones

Table of Contents

Chapter 1: Meet Michael A. Delitala

First and foremost, I'm no subject matter expert. That said, I'm extremely experienced in the Pharma Industry. Recently, my position at a big pharma company was eliminated. This is happening a lot in all industries. I was fortunate enough to find myself gainfully employed again at the same rank, making more money, having less responsibility and without any lapse in pay or benefits, and no longer have to commute being 100% remote.

Most of my colleagues and friends are finding themselves in dire straits. Anyway, as a new employee starting out again with a company for about the eighth or ninth time, I find myself growing overly fatigued with having to build equity at each new company I start over with. My goal is to not ever have to start over with another company ever again. (I state this very humbly because I do feel fortunate that I'm part of an organization where I can bring a quality and compliance mindset to protect patients and product).

I've been in the industry since 1995.

As of this writing that means I'm ancient and I have put in a dedicated twenty-nine years.

I've worked pre-clinical bench scale. In fact, I worked at bench scale for the U.S. Army but I can't tell you much more than that because it's Top Secret. That's not a joke. I can tell you that my work landed me a Meritorious Service Medal which is one of the highest awards one can obtain during peace. Basically, I was a "lab guy" and back then, Polyermase Chain Reactions (PCR) were "new". I hope you're laughing.

At the end of my four year enlistment, I had a choice: "You're either going to Bosnia, or you're going to Korea". I wanted neither of those! I decided to exit the military and pursued a Bachelor of Science in Sports Medicine, with a focus on physiology at Eastern Michigan University.

After I completed the degree in 2.5 years, I landed a job as a Quality Control Vaccine Lead.   This was with a company that was a very small contract manufacturing organization which meant I had the unique opportunity to "wear all the hats" as we like to say in the industry. I was Quality Control (Micro & Analytical), Manufacturing, and Quality Assurance. We manufactured early and late phase clinical trial biologics vaccines for viruses that at that time had no medicine for. (many of them still do not).

Wearing all of the hats gives you a lot of experience and in short order so that you become diverse. It's unusual to start a career getting experience in all aspects of pharma. For me, that's a critical point to make because we all grow up differently in quality and so each individual's experiences makes them who they are as a quality representative. In very short order in my early career I became exposed to deviations, CAPAs, change controls, all of the quality control micro tests, all of the quality control analytical tests, manufactured, learned tissue culture techniques, reviewed batch records, and even made disposition decisions.

As the QC guy I started to have feelings of boredom due to the repetitive nature of QC testing. Follow the test instructions, report the results, write laboratory investigation reports and blah blah blah. That said, I also discovered even though my resume had a list of a plethora of lab experiences, that companies were not interested in me because although I had a BS, I didn't have the right degree relevant to my lab experiences in the military. My resume said I could do xyz, but for pharma companies there was not a degree to back it up. I'm calling BS (see what I did there) Ok, fair enough…

I landed a job in Lansing, Michigan as a Quality Systems Deviation and CAPA Specialist for a commercial biologics vaccine company. Because I have a lot of energy, naturally, I enrolled in Michigan State University to obtain a Professional Master of Science in Biomedical Laboratory Operations. I completed all the course work while I was living in Lansing but I did not actually complete the degree while in Lansing. I spent many years at the Lansing facility and gained experience in Quality Assurance Operations (batch record review, release of raw materials, drug substance, and drug product), Quality Systems (deviation, CAPA & change control) and ended up being able to take on a supervisory role thank you to the individual that this volume is dedicated to. At this company, I also gained a lot of experience in Regulatory Inspections. I also had my first experience providing quality oversight to a contracted filler.

Then, I took the first biggest career risk and moved to Seal Beach, California for a novel Sipuleucel-T immunotherapy product. It was the first commercial immunotherapy product of its kind. It was clinical when I arrived, and it was one of my first priorities to make us commercial and also inspection ready. I was the Quality Systems Supervisor, but because of the short expiry of the product, I found myself in the manufacturing suites a lot, and also helping with batch record reviews. I wasn't informed ahead of taking the job that I would be working the night shift. My wife and I were maybe married three months at the time and so this became "bad news". Being on the night shift, I gave the company two dedicated years. And since I couldn't sleep during the day because we lived in the heart of downtown Long Beach, I used the day-time opportunity to finish my thesis. After two months of working tirelessly, I finally completed the requirements for and also graduated with the Professional Master of Science in Biomedical Laboratory Operations.

As soon as I received the degree and posted as such to my LinkedIn page I was nearly immediately recruited and hired by a large pharma company in Thousand Oaks, California. I was full quality oversight for three small molecule clinical manufacturing plants. The full circle of quality life as I like to say. One and half years from the start of the position and the company announced a major lay-off. I learned that the Site Program Owner for Deviation/CAPA was taking the package, so I volunteered to be the new Site Program Owner for Deviation/CAPA. It came with a high price because my new boss also charged me with being the Site Program Owner for Change Control and Quality Management Review. Mind you, this was for a company with >5000 employees at the site (all of which were customers in some regard relative to those programs). I also somehow found myself being the Program Owner for Deviation Trending. All of this in Quality Systems and far far away from anything production or product related.

It's easy to get lost in big pharma and I found myself wanting a change and a challenge (and a promotion!). I moved on to the next novel immunotherapy, a CAR-T company which also was the first of its kind. At this institution I felt like an "inventor" because I was asked to invent new procedures and new ways of working. I found that CAR-T was quite unique and that might be another volume of QbD someday. Anyway, I was globally responsible for Deviation, CAPA, Effectiveness Check, Change Control, and Quality Management Review. I was even the interim Head of the Quality Management System for greater than half of a year. I became a Project Lead and Business Lead to implement a new Quality Management System. Actually, implementing a new quality management system is something that follows me each time I join a company.

Which brings me to my current place of employment (as of this writing). Again, a novel product being a RNA Therapeutic where I'm the Lead of Quality Systems and Compliance.

I've trained more than 5000 trainees on Deviation, CAPA, EV, Root Cause Analysis, Change Control, Quality Management Review, and Training (training staff to be trainers).

I've participated in nearly 350 Regulatory Inspections as a SME and "Escort" with all regulatory bodies except the Asian Market. I'm known as "The Closer" in inspections and it's been since 2008 since I've received an observation on any of the quality systems I own or author (not bragging or ego there, but it is exceptional).

 I'm no expert but I'm highly experienced in all of the following:

QC Microbiology	QC Analytical	Tissue Culture
Lab Management	QA Operations	Work Order Review
Batch Record Review	BD – Raw Materials	BD-Intermediates
BD-Drug Substance	BD-Drug Product	BD-Immunotherapy
BD-Small Molecule	Lab Investigations	Computer Systems Validation
Equipment Qualification	Facility Qualification	Process Validation
Deviation Expert (Trending too)	CAPA Expert	Change Control Expert
Quality Management Review	EMQR	Trainer
Trainer of Trainers	Quality Risk Management	Risk Assessment
Technical Writer	SOP Author & Approver	Policy Author & Approver

BD = Batch Disposition   EMQR = Executive Management Quality Review   SOP = Standard Operating Procedure

In an attempt to succinctly summarize the whole of my experiences, I've worked pre-clinical bench scale, clinical phase 1, 2, and 3 in small molecule and biologics, clinical and commercial immunotherapy, and clinical (soon to be commercial) RNA Therapeutic. I've never worked in Medical Device and I hope I never do. I love the inherent variability of biologics and no offense to you Medical Device folks, it's just not for me. (CAPA before Deviation! Yuck! Micro iterations of change with intentionally planning to revert it back to the original state, again, Yuck!).

Chapter 2: What's the point?

By now, I hope you're wondering: Why am I reading this? What's the point of this drabble?

In short, I hope you have the opinion that I might actually be qualified to write about this subject.

I'm going to be very direct.

I'm writing this book because I want to give the world the answer. I want Quality employees that are new to the industry to have easy digestible reference material so that it makes their understanding of what "quality" is supposed to mean, expedited. For example, being exceptional with grammar is not "quality". That said, there are a plethora of resources that define "quality" so I'm not intending to "go there". Anyway, I want to give the answer away because conferences and consultants are expensive.

Also, I'm sick and tired of joining a company as a new employee thinking this will be the time I get to do this the way I want to do it. Inevitably I report to some supervisor who wants it their way and it's not the best that it can be and I don't settle for less than the best. So, it usually becomes a problem (for me and my "performance") because I'll provide excellent and then have it shredded to less than. (And of course you have to support the supervisor).

Also, start-up pharma companies or even the established commercial pharma companies do not need to keep hiring expensive consulting firms to write the book of policies and procedures. The tome of policies and procedures has largely been in place since the 1950's. So let's not kid ourselves any longer big consulting firms!

Finally, the market right now is tumultuous. There are massive lay-offs and those without employment are becoming desperate. I interviewed a candidate for a position that my current company is hiring for. She was laid off from a big pharma company. She started a consulting business. Then, that big pharma company hired her back as a consultant for the role that they eliminated her from. This does not make sense.

I will likely write a volume for each experience listed in the table above.

Deviation will be the next volume!

Now comes my legal disclaimer:

My mind is a trap. Think of the guy on Suits who can remember the page and sentence placement for a specific word. My brain works somewhat like that (unfortunately). For example, I can remember the procedure number for the Good Documentation SOP from a place I worked in 2004. So, for every company that I have worked for, please remember that you had me author a plethora of policies, standard operating procedures, work instructions, logs, forms, job aids, quick reference guides, training materials, investigations, CAPAs, EVs, Change Controls, and Quality Management Reviews. "That said, what I author in this book is from my brain, intellectual property, experience, invention, and how I would write anything if I were still working for you or the Head of Quality". Get it? It is 100% my work product. It is 100% my intellectual property (albeit that I'm giving it away for a small sum.)

Also, for the company that I am currently employed by…I authored this outside of working hours, generally at night during the week, on vacation days, or on weekends.

Large consultant firms and perhaps even the industry personified itself will hate me for this.

And I'm okay with that.

Now, if you're just here for the answer and don't care about the "what" or the "why" of The Quality Manual, skip ahead to Appendix 1. There in Appendix 1, I authored my version of the Quality Manual. Since you bought the book, you might be in need of the answer. I hope your boss thinks it's excellent work product (but they'll probably shared 😊 it!).

Good luck, and enjoy.

You're welcome to connect with me on LinkedIn:

www.linkedin.com/in/michaeldelitala

My intent is to keep this volume short.

No reason to be superfluous for the Quality Manual.

Volume 2, Deviation, should be extensive.

Chapter 3: What's required?

Many other reference materials like this one will detail for you every single regulation from all regulatory bodies where the Quality Manual is referenced. That certainly is an approach. My source of truth and my approach is to mostly pay attention to and reference the "Guidance for Industry Q10 Pharmaceutical Quality System".

Why: The Introduction of ICHQ10 explains that if you meet these guidance requirements, then you'll be compliant.

Two things here about what compliance means:

1. Compliance means following the regulations (the law).
2. Compliance also means meeting your own internal standards which are the company's policies and standard operating procedures.

I once had a clinical non-quality leader tell my quality leadership that "that new Delitala guy is holding us to a higher standard than we are used to". My response was, "There is a book of SOPs that existed before I joined the organization that you all authored and approved. I'm just pointing out that we're not following them". After that, I helped them be more phase-appropriate with their SOPs which were written to a commercial standard. And as I like to say, simplicity breeds compliance.

If anyone comes at you with, "this is out of compliance", remember what compliance means and politely challenge their assertion that 1) either we've broken the law or 2) we've departed from our own internal standard. Usually, they just have a problem to work through, and as the quality partner, it helps when Quality understands the business so that Quality (proper) can separate the emotion of being out of compliance with the logic of helping with the problem.

Also, "guidance" = law. Europeans are more polite than the FDA and even though it says "guidance" it's really law. The FDA goes in to inspect you and they are trained to look for non-compliance and spank you with 483 Observations if they've determined you have broken a law. I would be remiss if I didn't mention that this process protects us as patients and those of us who take prescription medicine or over the counter medicine. Ok! So, we need them and just in case you don't agree with that please go ahead and google "the thalidomide tragedy". The Europeans come in and say, "hey, we think you could do this better, and here's how". So, they will still write you up, but they're nice about it and they tend to offer a solution. No offense FDA. I could write a little about IGJ, TGA, Ministry of Health, Health Canada, ANVISA, and Turkish Medicines and Medical Device Agency as well.

I digress. Please continue below for what ICHQ10 requires for the Quality Manual.

ICHQ10 Quality Manual:

<table><tr><td>

A Quality Manual or equivalent documentation approach should be established and should contain the description of the pharmaceutical quality system. The description should include:
1. The *quality policy*
2. The scope of the pharmaceutical quality system.
3. Identification of the pharmaceutical quality system process, as well as their sequences, linkages, and interdependencies. Process maps and flow charts can be useful tools to facilitate depicting pharmaceutical quality system processes in a visual manner.
4. Management responsibilities within the pharmaceutical quality system.

</td></tr></table>

ICHQ10 Quality Policy

1. *Senior Management* should establish a quality policy that describes the overall intentions and direction of the company related to quality.
2. The quality policy should include an expectation to comply with applicable regulatory requirements and should facilitate continual improvement of the pharmaceutical quality system.
3. The quality policy should be communicated to and understood by personnel at all levels in the company.
4. The quality policy should be reviewed periodically for continuing effectiveness.

ICHQ10 Management Responsibilities (Senior Management)

1. Senior management has the ultimate responsibility to ensure an effective pharmaceutical quality system is in place to achieve the quality objectives, and that roles, responsibilities, and authorities are defined, communicated, and implemented throughout the company.
- Senior Management is defined as Person(s) who direct and control a company or site at the highest levels with the authority and responsibility to mobilize resources within the company or site.

ICHQ10 Management

Management should:
1. Participate in the design, implementation, monitoring, and maintenance of an effective pharmaceutical quality system.
2. Demonstrate strong and visible support for the pharmaceutical quality system and ensure its implementation throughout their organization.
3. Ensure a timely and effective communication and escalation process exists to raise quality issues to the appropriate levels of management.
4. Define individual and collective roles, responsibilities, authorities, and interrelationships of all organizational units related to the

pharmaceutical quality system. Ensure these interactions are communicated and understood at all levels of the organization. An independent quality unit / structure with authority to fulfill certain pharmaceutical quality system responsibilities is required by regional regulations.
5. Conduct management reviews of process performance and product quality and of the pharmaceutical quality system.
6. Advocate continual improvement.
7. Commit appropriate resources.

What is this thing they keep referring to as the *pharmaceutical quality system*? It's defined in ICHQ10 as "The management system to direct and control a pharmaceutical company with regard to quality". What it means is that a company has to have a specific set of controls in place to ensure that reliably and consistently, a patient will receive a product that is safe, of the right potency, of the right efficacy, and that it has met all of its product quality attributes.

There are unique sets of controls put in place, they each have a quality system name, and per each quality system, it has an intended outcome. So, the Quality Manual defines each unique control and the whole makes up the pharmaceutical quality system.

In early stage pharma, the pharmaceutical quality system, which hereafter I will refer to as the Quality Management System (QMS), is governed by Policy and Procedure and is usually paper based. I mention this because most individuals think of a system as an application or a computer. In commercial pharma, the QMS is also governed by Policy and Procedure and is also usually contained in a Validated Computer System that is usually called the Quality Management System.

Hopefully I've provided clarity here that the QMS is a principle to ensure a company relative to quality is in a state of control. And, that the QMS is a computer system ensuring the same.

In reading through the above requirements here is how a Quality Manual is generally structured:

Section	Why
Introduction	• Defines who the company is and what they manufacture
Purpose	• Describes that it is the governing document ensuring through the QMS the company will remain in a state of control relative to product quality
Scope	• Informs of how in-sourced vs out-sourced activities are managed
Company Mission	• Defines what the company is committed to
Responsibilities of Senior Management	• Accountability (because the law says so)
Document Hierarchy	• Defines the levels and categories of documents and records to support the QMS.
Continuous Improvement	• Defines the methodology by which systems, processes, or products can be improved through data insights.　(Which means the company also has to collect data.)
The QMS	• In full, the define the QMS:　Compliance, Documentation System and Controls, Electronic Records & Data Integrity etc etc. • Why:　This sets the stage for a Regulator at your attempt to be compliant to the law.　(It's really that simple!)

That's it.　Of course, you'll have to adapt the below to meet your company's needs.　I've created an example company to provide the manual.　No reason to continue to wax poetic.　The End.

Appendix 1: The Quality Manual by Quality by Delitala (QbD)

Title: Quality Manual

Table of Contents

1. Introduction
2. Purpose
3. Scope
4. Company Mission
5. Quality Policy
6. Management Responsibility
7. Quality Unit Responsibility
8. Document Hierarchy
9. Continuous Improvement
10. Outsourced Activities
11. Quality Management System Framework & Quality Processes
    a. Table 1- Processes that Ensure the Health of the QMS
    b. Table 2 – Processes that Ensure the Control of the QMS
    c. Table 3 – Processes for the Lifecycle of the QMS
12. Knowledge Management
13. Quality Plan

1. Introduction

Callirrhoe Biosciences (Callirrhoe) is a biopharmaceutical company that develops and commercializes innovative drug substance and drug product in areas of unmet medical needs to overcome the limitations and improve the quality of life for those with a rare disease.

Callirrhoe's Quality Management System is based on the International Conference on Harmonization (ICHQ10) guidelines and regulatory requirements and expectations from Regulatory Bodies such as the Food and Drug Administration (FDA), European Medicines Agency (EMA), Therapeutic Goods Agency (TGA), Health Canada, Brazilian Health

Regulatory Agency (ANVISA), Inspection General of Justice (IGJ) and others.

The ICHQ10 guidelines describe the modern quality system elements necessary to facilitate the development, continuous monitoring of, and continuous improvement of a medicinal product over the product's lifecycle. The ICH "Q" (quality) elements augment the current Good Manufacturing Practices (cGMP) regulations.

Callirrhoe operates mostly in an outsourced business model by which manufacturing, testing, and distribution are performed by contract service organizations (CSO). Callirrhoe has oversight and governance practices in place by which Callirrhoe maintains overall responsibility for the compliance of the activities completed by CSOs. The only activity not outsourced to a CSO is where Callirrhoe maintains a GMP Raw Materials Warehouse located in Thousand Oaks, California.

Callirrhoe mandates continuous improvement of its quality management system and takes pride in ensuring continuous supply of high-quality products to patients that are safe and effective.

2. Purpose

The purpose of this Quality Manual is to define the framework and requirements for Callirrhoe's Quality Management System (QMS). It is Callirrhoe's guiding document intended for the overall planning, administration, and execution of all Callirrhoe's GxP related activities. This manual defines the procedures and philosophy that are practiced by Callirrhoe's personnel to ensure compliance during the development, manufacture, testing, storage, and distribution throughout the product lifecycle as referenced in ICHQ10.

The Quality Manual is designed to accomplish three main objectives:

- **Product Realization:** Establish, implement, and maintain a system that enables the delivery of products with the quality attributes appropriate to meet the needs of patients, Regulatory Bodies, and other internal or external stakeholders.

- **Establish and Maintain a State of Control as Defined in ICHQ10.**
- **Facilitate Continuous Improvement:** Examples include variation reduction, quality by design during process validation and equipment qualification, product quality improvements, innovations, and quality system enhancements.

3. Scope

This Quality Manual applies to commercial and investigational products manufactured and distributed throughout the product lifecycle. This Quality Manual applies to all Callirrhoe's employees responsible for product development, technology transfer, manufacturing, testing, labeling, packaging, distributing, and managing commercial and investigational products for human use. All of Callirrhoe's contractors, consultants, or suppliers are also in the scope of this Quality Manual as agreed to via contract and quality agreements.

4. Company Mission

To preserve and improve patient's health by consistently delivering high quality, safe, and effective pharmaceutical products and services that meet customer expectations across the globe through current good manufacturing practices, state of the art technology, competent workforce, and efficient management.

5. Quality Policy

Callirrhoe's QMS ensures that the development, manufacture, and distribution of our products are completed in a manner that is compliant to all applicable regulations and our internal company standards.

Callirrhoe maintains an independent Quality Unit to assure that the defined QMS is effective through measurable objectives.

Processes and programs are in place to ensure that quality and compliance top risks and noncompliance are escalated and reported to management timely for swift resolution so as to not adversely impact patient safety.

Callirrhoe is committed to delivering products that are safe and effective.

6. Management Responsibility

Callirrhoe's Executive Management is committed to ensuring a company-wide commitment to quality and for the performance of the QMS. In this regard, Quality is an independent functional area.

Management Must:

- Participate in the design, implementation, monitoring, and maintenance of an effective pharmaceutical quality system.
- Demonstrate strong and visible support for the pharmaceutical quality system and ensure its implementation throughout their organization.
- Ensure a timely and effective communication and escalation process exists to raise quality issues to the appropriate levels of management.
- Define individual and collective roles, responsibilities, authorities, and interrelationships of all organizational units related to the pharmaceutical quality system. Ensure these interactions are communicated and understood at all levels of the organization.
- Conduct management reviews of process performance and product quality and of the pharmaceutical quality system.
- Advocate for continual improvement.
- Commit appropriate resources.

7. Quality Unit Responsibility

Quality is the responsibility of every Callirrhoe employee.

The Quality Unit is the independent authority to approve and reject materials and products when there is impact to safety, identity, strength, purity, and quality (SISPQ)

The Quality Unit is the responsible and independent authority to ensure that all process and testing-related activities are performed according to the intended purpose and identified standards.

The Quality Unit is the only authority to review and approve all product release data and perform the final product release through the Quality defined review and disposition process.

Callirrhoe employs Quality Persons (QP) and Responsible Persons (RP) to verify and certify that each product released to an applicable international jurisdiction has been manufactured and checked in accordance with marketing and/or clinical trial authorization, relevant regulations, and specifications.

8.   Document Hierarchy

The Document Hierarchy defines the levels and sublevels of documents and records in support of the QMS. This is a key structural component to be in a state of control as defined in ICHQ10. Refer to the below figure for the Callirrhoe Document Hierarchy.

Figure 1 – QMS Document Hierarchy

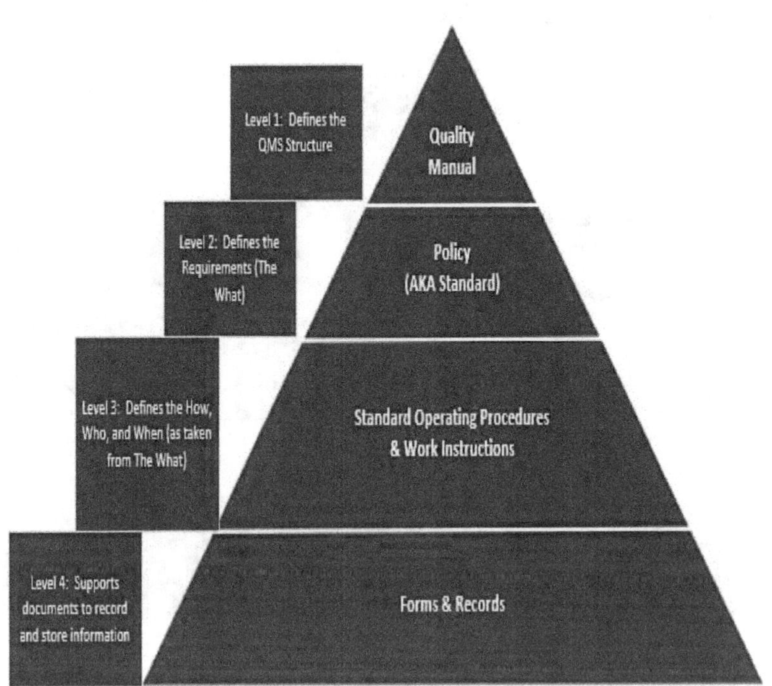

9. Continuous Improvement

Callirrhoe promotes continuous improvement throughout the whole of the QMS. Continuous improvement is promoted and achieved through the evaluation of data by the executive management, which provides insights on business or compliance topics. Of which the evaluation leads to initiatives, projects, or governance forums ensuring that something that needs an improvement is actually improved. Refer to Figure 2 for Callirrhoe's process in promoting continuous improvement. Callirrhoe also maintains the QMS with enabling programs such Quality Risk Management and Knowledge Management. Additionally, Callirrhoe subscribes to the Plan-Do-Check-Act (PDCA) cycle.

Figure 2 – Continuous Improvement Callirrhoe's QMS

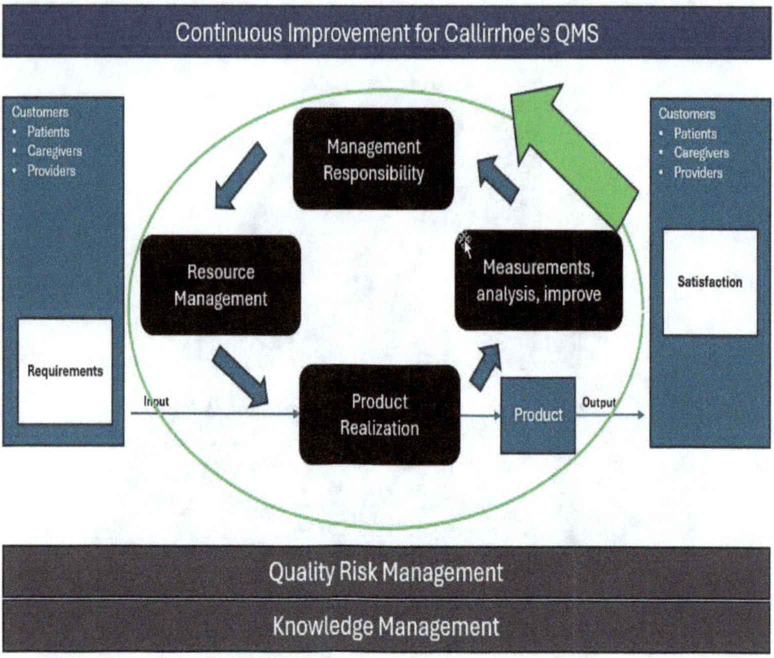

10. Outsourced Activities

Callirrhoe maintains oversight and is ultimately responsible for all GxP outsourced activities.

Callirrhoe ensures compliance with relevant regulations and internal Callirrhoe standards by having robust outsourced vendor selection, qualification, and oversight monitoring programs.

Callirrhoe defines the relationship between Callirrhoe and Contract Service Organizations (CSO) in contracts, agreements, Master Service Agreements (MSA), Scope of Work (SoW), Non-Disclosure Agreements (NDAs) and / or any other contractual arrangement between Callirrhoe & a CSO.

11. Quality Management System Framework and Quality Processes

Callirrhoe's QMS consists of Quality Processes that are used to translate quality & regulatory requirements into a defined hierarchy. The Quality Processes are integrated throughout the product lifecycle to meet critical product quality attributes and exceed regulatory compliance. At Callirrhoe, each Quality Process requires management oversight and accountability to timeliness, resources, and defined escalation and decision-making methodologies.

The Health of the QMS is evaluated and defined with a policy and a procedure for Corrective Action Preventive Action (CAPA), Deviation management, Internal Audits maintaining Regulatory Inspection Readiness, Quality Risk Management, and Quality Management Review. Refer to Table 1.

Table 1 – Processes that Ensure the Health of the QMS

Health of the QMS	
Process	**High Level Description**
CAPA (POL-0000XXX)	The CAPA program has several source quality inputs to correct or prevent quality issues and is the framework for continuous improvement. Inputs include but are not limited to Deviations, Product Complaints, Quality Management Review, Internal Audits, and Regulatory Inspections. Effectiveness Verifications are required at Callirrhoe in a risk based manner.
Deviation Management (POL-0000XXX)	Departures from Policy, Procedure, or atypical events will be documented as deviations, classified in a risk based manner and will determine the following outputs: Impact to Product, Root Cause, and Actionable CAPA.
	Internal GxP functions are audited at defined frequencies against the full of the QMS for quality performance and compliance to promote continuous improvement and maintain regulatory inspection readiness. The program also includes audits of suppliers, partner audits, and surveillance of regulatory observations issued to competitors.
Quality Risk Management (QRM) (POL-0000XXX)	QRM is an enabler ensuring ICHQ10 is implemented effectively and successively. QRM is a proactive approach to identifying, evaluating, controlling or mitigating potential or actual risks to product quality which facilitates continual improvement of process performance and product quality through the lifecycle. Often, QRM is the means to define science and decisions from science related to product quality.
Quality Management Review (POL-0000XXX)	Quality Management Review will assess the QMS for effectiveness and suitability using established criteria for metrics and key performing indicators encompassing the full of the QMS ensuring that Callirrhoe is in a state of control as defined by ICHQ10. Other components include Quality Issue Escalation and Annual Product Review.

The Control of the QMS is evaluated and defined with a policy and a procedure for Change Management, Data Integrity, Document & Records Management, Managing Suppliers & Service Providers, and Personnel Qualification & Training. Refer to Table 2.

Table 2 – Processes that Ensure the Control of the QMS

Control of the QMS	
Process	**High Level Description**
Change Management (Control) (POL-0000XXX)	Change Management (Change Control) assesses all changes to ensure that changes will not alter anything GxP without unintended consequences and prevent variation. At Callirrhoe, changes that are controlled are manufacturing or testing changes, specification revisions, computerized systems, labels, and controlled documents with any filing impact. The system applies to process, material, equipment, facility, specification or any such item that requires qualification or validation.
Data Integrity (POL-0000XXX)	Data Integrity at Callirrhoe begins with good documentation practices. Data management governance forums are established. Data collection and storage are explicitly defined and is the responsibility of every Callirrhoe employee. Callirrhoe governs electronic data handling and audit trails and requires all GxP computerized systems to be 21 CFR Part 11 compliant.
Document & Records Management (Control) (POL-0000XXX)	Document & Records Management (Document Control) requires a document change control strategy to evaluate any changes to not only the impact of the document but also to the documents that are dependent upon it. The program governs the controlled document lifecycle, periodic document review, document storage, archiving & retention, and electronic records.

Control of the QMS	
Process	**High Level Description**
Managing Suppliers & Service Providers (POL-0000XXX)	Callirrhoe maintains oversight and is ultimately responsible for all GxP outsourced activities. Callirrhoe ensures compliance of relevant regulations and internal Callirrhoe standards by having a robust outsourced vendor selection, qualification, and oversight monitoring programs. Callirrhoe defines the relationship between Callirrhoe and Contract Service Organizations (CSO) in contracts, agreements, Master Service Agreements (MSA), Scope of Work (SoW), Non-Disclosure Agreements (NDAs) and / or any other contractual arrangement between Callirrhoe & a CSO.
Personnel Qualification & Training (POL-0000XXX)	All Callirrhoe's employees (full time staff, part time staff, contract workers, and consultants) are trained and qualified through a combination of education, experience, on-the-job (OJT) training, web-based-training, and read/understand of GxP controlled documents in order to execute assigned job functions which are documented and controlled through a job description. All Callirrhoe's employees have a quality maintained and archived training file which includes the employee's curriculum vitae (resume).

The Lifecycle of the QMS is evaluated and defined with a policy and a procedure for the remainder of the QMS. Note: Policy and Procedure are required for each Process and each bullet of the process (the short description). Refer to Table 3.

Table 3 – Processes for the Lifecycle of the QMS

Control of the QMS	
Process	**Short Description**
Batch Review & Disposition	<ul><li>Full review of the requirements to decide if Raw Material, Intermediates, Drug Substance, Drug Product etc may be released, rejected or quarantined.</li></ul>
Contamination Control	<ul><li>Process monitoring</li><li>Microbiological control</li><li>Aseptic process validation</li><li>Aseptic Operator qualification</li><li>Environmental monitoring program</li><li>In process controls</li></ul>
Facilities & Equipment Maintenance	<ul><li>Facility design, unplanned shutdowns, and business continuity</li><li>Calibration, preventive maintenance, management of out of frequencies and out of tolerances.</li><li>Cleaning & Disinfecting.</li><li>Access and Security</li><li>Pest Control</li></ul>
Label & Labeling Control	<ul><li>Artwork and Label Specifications</li><li>Labels, Labeling Receipt, Label Storage, Label Inspection and Label Disposition.</li><li>Label design, development, qualification, approval, and filing.</li><li>Label printing, issuance, review, disposition, and accountability.</li></ul>
Laboratory Controls	<ul><li>Equipment and Instrument calibration, qualification</li><li>Sampling and Sampling plans</li><li>Reagents, Reference Standards</li><li>Test Methods</li><li>USP Compendial Methods</li><li>Laboratory Investigations</li><li>Out of Specifications Results Management</li><li>Contract Laboratory Testing</li></ul>
Material Controls	<ul><li>Material Selection and Handling</li><li>Material Specification</li></ul>

	• Material Sampling and Testing

Table 3 Continued – Processes for the Lifecycle of the QMS

Control of the QMS	
Process	**Short Description**
Process / Product Development and Design & Production Controls	• Data Management • Quality Requirements for data generation for future filings • Manufacturing Records • Performance Monitoring • Contamination control for multi-product facilities • Critical Utility qualification • Technology Transfer
Product Complaints	• Product Complaint Management • Adverse Event Management
Recalls	• Product Recall & Market Withdrawal
Regulatory Reporting	• Regulatory Notification Assessment (such as Biological Product Deviation Reporting)
Specification Lifecycle Management	• Specification development, justification, creating, approval, and change as controlled through change management. • Evaluation of specification changes on past batches, in-process batches, and forecasted batches.
Stability	• Shelf-life expiry establishment • Study Design • Stability Evaluation and Reporting
Supply Chain Security	• Intellectual Property Security • Risk Management of External Suppliers, vendors, logistics, and transportation
Warehousing and Distribution	• Control of Materials • Procurement and Logistics • Third Party Distributers
Qualification & Validation	• Validation Master Planning & Validation Periodic Review • Qualification and Validation of equipment and processes • Periodic Review (is the thing still in a state of qualification or validation) • Decommissioning

12. Knowledge Management

Note to you, Dear Reader. In my twenty-nine years in the industry, I have only observed one large pharma company that has a program and a policy in place for Knowledge Management. I predict that Regulators will start to pull the thread and start issuing observations for not having a Knowledge Management program or policy. Why: Because it's stated very clearly in ICHQ10 that Knowledge Management is a key enabler to implementing the QMS effectively and successfully. That said, I'm sure your boss will nix this section should you choose to include it. Here's what my version would say:

Callirrhoe has a Knowledge Management program, policy, and system that ensures there is a systematic approach to acquire, analyze, store, and disseminate information related to products, manufacturing, processes, and components. This is achieved in great part via Callirrhoe's Quality Management Review and Callirrhoe's Executive Management Quality Review. Additionally, Callirrhoe publishes a monthly quality newsletter that reaches the full organization. Sources of knowledge management are Callirrhoe's personnel, designs of experiments, technology transfers, process validation, experience, innovation, continuous improvement activities, change management, industry journals, industry forums, and scientific publications.

13. Quality Plan

Callirrhoe has a Quality Plan as a controlled document that defines and communicates the objectives related to improving the QMS, product, and compliance to regulatory requirements. The Quality Plan aligns to Callirrhoe's objectives and strategies to bring product to market. The Quality Plan is reviewed and approved by Callirrhoe's Executive Management and is communicated from the top down and becomes part of Callirrhoe's personnel yearly goals.

Appendix 2 – A Note Regarding the Dedication

Emergent BioSolutions in Lansing, Michigan will always hold a special place in my thoughts and heart. I was an employee there for six or so years and in that time I had six or so supervisors. All of them were great, by the way. That said, Jefferey T. Jones stands out, even today, after more than two decades of working elsewhere, as the best supervisor I have ever had. (He's blushing right now if he's reading this).

When I met Jeff, I was an individual contributor serving as the Change Control Lead. The Change Control Lead was the sole quality reviewer and gatekeeper of all the change controls. In the two years I held the role I wrote the Quality Risk Assessment and determined for each change owner what the change actions were in order to implement the change. I kept track of the metrics for change controls and again, because my mind is a trap, I wrote or reviewed, and approved greater than 200 changes. Anyway, at the time I met Jeff, he was fairly new to the company and had been newly named the Head of Quality. My memory goes so far back on this topic that I actually remember being a part of the interview panel for the position and he stood out as my number 1. I was happy to see he had obtained the position.

It was about this time in my own personal development that I realized I had a superpower of noticeable pattern recognition. Prior to Jeff, I had observed three other Head's of Quality come and go for reasons that do not matter for this dedication. A pattern I observed was something I like to call the full circle of quality life (part 2). A Head of Quality is hired, they take about 90 days to see how everything is working, complete a full review of the QMS, then restructure the quality organization and change the full of the QMS. The comedy of the full circle of quality life is that in some manner or regard or fashion the QMS inevitably and invariably becomes the version of itself that it has already been once before. Observing this pattern…

After an all-quality staff meeting, I stalked Jeff and cornered him. I introduced myself with a firm handshake and explained to him what my current role was. Jeff is an introvert and my impression was that this was a tad unusual for him (like, who does this!). I said, "Jeff, I'm so very happy you decided to join this organization and I look forward to working with you. One thing: If you decide that the quality organization is in need of a restructure, I would very much like you to consider moving me into a supervisory position. I think I could be more valuable to you somewhere like in Quality Systems or Quality Operations. In any regard, I'm more than an individual contributor. As I was previously a leader of a platoon in the military, I believe I really need an opportunity to lead staff in the industry to be promoted later and I have the skills to do so. Because after all, I aspire to someday have your position".

A few months go by. I don't recall if Jeff and I had any interactions after that. As I said, he's an introvert and he was probably busy doing all those things I mentioned that good leaders do in their first 90 days.

Then, a quality all staff meeting is announced. No one had any ideas what the agenda was going to be. And in this meeting, Jeff announces a restructure of the quality organization. One of the main announcements and a shocking surprise to all in the room, including myself, was that Jeff said, "Effective Immediately, Mike Delitala will be promoted to Quality Assurance Supervisor, in charge of Quality Assurance Operations on the commercial aspect. Mike will have eight direct reports will take on Raw Material release, Intermediate Release, sublot (drug substance release), and drug product release. Please, let's take a moment to congratulate Mike". Clapping ensued, although there were a few people in the room that, after the meeting, pointed their finger in my face and literally said, "you better not fuck this up!". When Jeff and I spoke later in the day, he said, "Mike, in all of my years, I have never had anyone walk up to me as confident as you were, and volunteer themselves to move into management. It was impressive and told me a lot about your character".

Jeff and I reminisce about something specific that happens between us every so often. He'll change his phone number and then text me saying, "you've still made the cut in being in my personal contacts. Oh by the way, this is Jeff Jones". I'll say, "Jeff prove to me that you're the Jeff Jones that I know".

"Mike, and I'm not proud of this to this very day. One day you came into my office. I was busy with something that was a high priority and my boss needed it like yesterday. You were whining about this or that, I don't remember anymore. I looked at you dead in your face. I said, 'Well, do you stand by your own decision'.

"Yes", I said.

"Well, Mike, then get the fuck over it and the fuck out of my office".

I remember, laughing out loud really hard. Asked Jeff if he was serious. He said he was. And I thought to myself, and maybe even said out loud. Ok then, I will get the fuck over it, and thank you for supporting me and my decision. And for all the years that I have followed, it was exactly what I needed to hear, and I have since *gotten the fuck over it* time and time again.

All of this is to say that Jeff knew me. We went through a horrific FDA inspection where my department received the majority of the 483 Observations. Jeff gave me profound advice that no matter how productive I was that I would not be able to achieve the response to and complete the work necessary to remediate the observations. "Form a team, Mike. You're going to need to form a team. You've got 30 days to change 12 processes. I believe you're the only one capable of being able to do this in the time you have".

And he was right. We did it in 28 days as a matter of fact. And it stands as one of my proudest achievements to this day.

I could be wrong, but I might have been the only individual to point out to Jeff that in the signature line of his email, he had made the period a different color compared to all of the other characters in this signature line. Something like this: Jefferey T. Jones. "Jeff did you do that intentionally"?

"I sure did Mike." Then we both just looked at each other and smiled.

Jeff, as my supervisor and friend you set me on the path to be "more" and once even asked me "why aren't you already in California? That's where I see you".

Thank you, dear friend. This volume is dedicated to you. I hope you enjoyed it.